A Quilted Memory

A Quilted Memory

Ideas and Inspiration for Reusing Vintage Textiles

Mary Kerr

Schiffer Publishing Ltd®

4880 Lower Valley Road, Atglen, Pennsylvania 19310

Dedication

To my mother,
Corene Wilson,
my first and most patient teacher

Corene Crissie Say, 1953

Another Schiffer Book By The Author:
A Quilt Block Challenge: Vintage Revisited.
ISBN:978-0-7643-3457-3. $24.99

Library of Congress Control Number: 2011936471

Designed by Mark David Bowyer
Type set in Modern20 BT / Zurich BT

ISBN: 978-0-7643-3921-9
Printed in China

Schiffer Books are available at special discounts for bulk purchases for sales promotions or premiums. Special editions, including personalized covers, corporate imprints, and excerpts can be created in large quantities for special needs. For more information contact the publisher:

Published by Schiffer Publishing Ltd.
4880 Lower Valley Road
Atglen, PA 19310
Phone: (610) 593-1777; Fax: (610) 593-2002
E-mail: Info@schifferbooks.com

For the largest selection of fine reference books on this and related subjects, please visit our website at
www.schifferbooks.com
We are always looking for people to write books on new and related subjects. If you have an idea for a book, please contact us at
proposals@schifferbooks.com

This book may be purchased from the publisher.
Include $5.00 for shipping.
Please try your bookstore first.
You may write for a free catalog.

In Europe, Schiffer books are distributed by
Bushwood Books
6 Marksbury Ave.
Kew Gardens
Surrey TW9 4JF England
Phone: 44 (0) 20 8392 8585; Fax: 44 (0) 20 8392 9876
E-mail: info@bushwoodbooks.co.uk
Website: www.bushwoodbooks.co.uk

Contents

Acknowledgments

Thank you to all who supported me as I have created this collection of memory pieces. I have been blessed to be able to share my quilts and stories with students, family members and a supportive network of friends. Thank you to all the talented quilters who gave me their best as they finished my pieces. They added another layer of magic to these quilts.

Thank you to Barb Garrett for her generous assistance with photography. Thank you to Laurie Moody, Nancy Buckler, and Karen Mitchell for reading the manuscripts in progress and helping to organize my thoughts. Thank you to my editor, Nancy Schiffer, and the staff at Schiffer Publishing, Ltd. for their encouragement and support.

Thank you to my mother, Corene Wilson, who spent hours going over all the family stories, photos, and linens. And last, but not least, thank you to my family and to the women in my life who serve as my army of cheerleaders. Life would not be the same without you!

Detail of *Party Time* (page 36).

Introduction

Memories are what tie us to our past. They are those special thoughts that wrap us in the warmth of family, friends and cherished moments. For me, the smell of cookies baking takes me back to my grandmother's kitchen. The sound of a favorite hymn sends my sisters and me back to family music sessions with our Daddy. The warmth of a patchwork quilt reminds me of the generations of women who have cherished and cared for us through the years.

As women, we are in a unique position. If your family is anything like mine, we tend to be the keepers of the traditions, and the ones who remember the important dates. We pass along the stories, rituals, recipes, and experiences. We know the faces in the old photos and we are driven to share this information with our children. I want them to hear the stories and share in my memories.

Henry Edmund Say, 1929

I am blessed to have grown up in a family of industrious women. Both of my grandmothers, my great-grandmothers, and my countless aunts were quilters. Those who did not quilt were accomplished needlewomen and their homes were full of embroidered linens, crocheted treasures, knitted scarves, and hand-work of every shape and size.

As these women have passed away, I have been given many pieces of their needlework. As the only grandchild from either side who followed a quilting path, I have been the proud recipient of most of their sewing ephemera, unfinished projects, damaged linens, and scrap bags. If someone did not know what to do with an item, it was passed on to me! Over the years, I found myself with a large collection of family pieces that were never used but were kept safe in trunks, boxes, and drawers.

The women in my family were frugal. As did many people of their generation, they repaired damaged items, repurposed rather than purchased new, and saved everything! They were children of the Depression and "making-do" was a life-long habit. Dresses were remade, fabrics were recycled, clothes were patched to last another season, and nothing went to waste. In their textiles we find feed sacks, used clothing, drapery scraps, and remnants from the shirt factory where my grandmother worked.

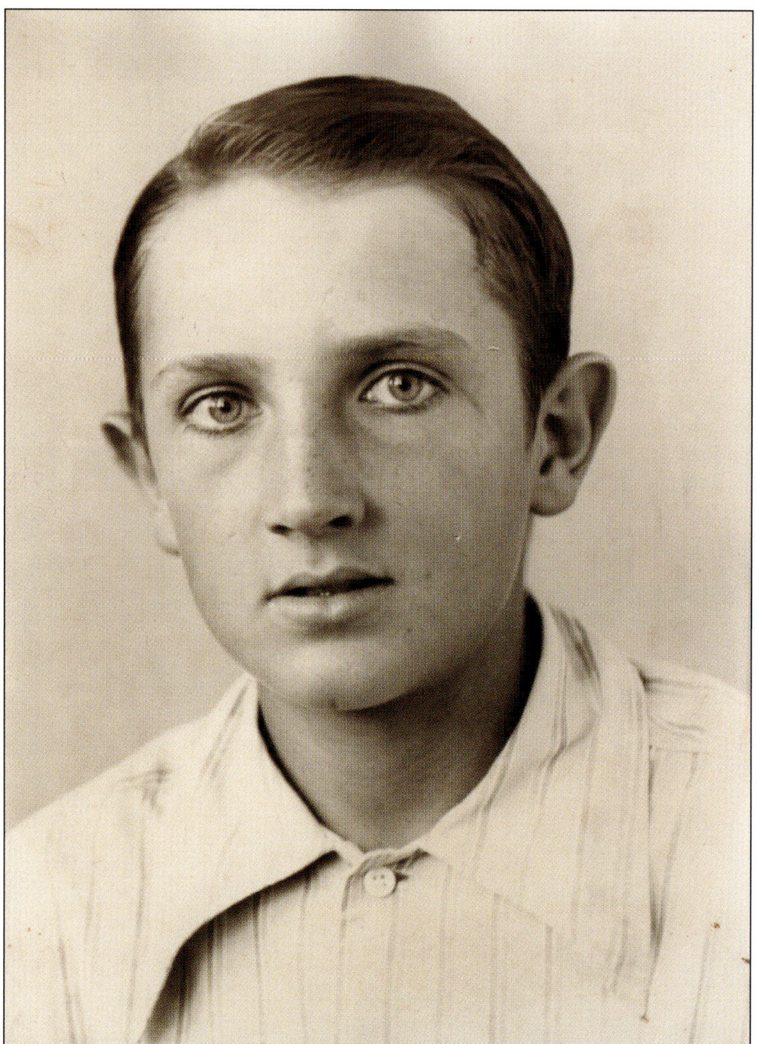

James William Wilson, 1949

Jim and Allie Wilson, 1902

I challenged myself to apply this same "make-do" mentality to create memory quilts for my family. I had articles of clothing, dresser scarves, handkerchiefs, fragments of unfinished projects, and lots of buttons. What would happen if I incorporated these vintage pieces into my contemporary wall hangings? How wonderful would it be to liberate these pieces from their storage bins and allow them to shine in a new and exciting way? Wouldn't the women who came before me smile to see their tradition of cherished recycling being passed on to a new generation?

With these quilts, I have found a way to save treasured textiles, honor their makers, and pass the stories on to my children and generations to come. I am thrilled to share my quilts in this book and I look forward to inspiring others to create their own Quilted Memories.

David and Nora Cummins 1908

My Inspirations

Kathyrne Elizabeth Pickering Say (July 27th, 1912 - December 23, 2003) was born in 1912, the third girl born to a family of seven. At the age of 18, she married Henry Say, who immediately shortened her name to Kay Say! Together they raised three girls and were married 64 years. She was a jack-of-all-trades: a hard-working farm wife who supplemented the family income as a hairdresser, a cook, and a riviter during World War II.

My Grandma Kay had the unique ability to make each of her ten grandchildren feel they were the most important persons in her life. Every one of us is convinced to this day that we were her favorite child! From her I learned to appreciate quilts, family, a mean game of cards, pink Depression glass, and homemade strawberry jam. My daughter Katherine is her namesake.

Kay passed away in 2003 at the age of 92, after a long struggle with Parkinson's Disease. Her body was failing but her mind remained clear and her sense of humor was legendary. I loved being able to share my latest quilting project with her and see the delight in her eyes as she watched me play with her fabric. I was blessed to be able to spend time with her.

Minnie Opal Cummins Wilson (March 8, 1912 - August 15, 2007) was born in 1912, the thirteenth child in a large blended family. Opal left home as a teenager and worked in various homes, until she married Harry Wilson in 1932. They raised two sons in Linwood, Kansas.

My Grandmother Opal is the one who actually sat down and taught me to quilt. I thought I knew what I was doing and limped along with sometimes disastrous results. I remember making two baby quilts for my sisters in the late 1980s, that would not lay flat nor look like I needed them to. Grandma Opal came to visit and we dissected those two quilts and reconstructed them while we butted heads and attempted to be more stubborn than the other.

Opal made countless quilts and quilted for others during her long career. We have estimated that she worked on over 300 quilts in her lifetime and was actively quilting until 2005. She was a talented needlewoman who crocheted, knitted, tatted, and sewed clothes for more people than we will ever know. The image of her was taken at her 95th birthday, in March of 2007. Until the week before she died, she was working with her hands and making sure we all stayed in line.

Kay Say and Katherine Kerr 2002

Minnie Opal Wilson 2007

Chapter One

Kitchen Linens

A typical kitchen in the early to mid-1900s was full of linens. Tablecloths, towels, aprons and napkins were necessary items in any well-run kitchen. They filled the drawers and decorated the space. These linens were embellished with embroidery, paint, cut-work, and fancy edgings. They provided a utilitarian canvas for beautiful needle skills. As our society progressed into the 1960s, we entered a world of paper towels and disposable napkins. The linens were put away: stored in trunks and closets. They were too pretty to dispose of, yet too archaic to continue using. Our current generation is now the fortunate recipient of this treasure trove of textiles. I choose to incorporate them into quilted creations and I challenge others to preserve their family memories by showcasing their treasured linens.

A Chicken from Wilsey

My Grandmother Kay created this wonderful painted tea towel that celebrated her love of chickens. She and my grandfather raised poultry; their barnyard was always full of feathered activity. Over the years, Kay collected dozens of ceramic and glass chickens of all shapes and sizes. I was not surprised to find this painted version in a box of linens from her estate. I paired this cheery towel with new black fabric and added fragments of a vintage star block from the 1890s.

Kay Say, 1931

Raw materials

32" x 32" Machine quilted by Shannon Shirley

A Rooster from Linwood

Shortly after the Wilsey chicken top was completed, I discovered another kitchen tea towel that celebrated our chickens. The second towel features a rooster appliquéd onto a black background, and it was created by my other grandmother, Opal Wilson. Two tea towels, two chickens, opposite color schemes, created by two, very different grandmothers! Needless to say, I was a bit excited and loved having the opportunity to finish them with the same star fragments.

The star blocks are typical of colors found in the late 1800s. I carefully "un-sewed" the large diamonds and appliquéd them onto the border using a fusible web. The use of commercial fusible allows me to use fabrics that are frequently too fragile to piece in the traditional manner. I fuse the product to the back of the vintage block and trim it to the size needed. The raw edges are held in place with the fusible web and machine-applied buttonhole stitches.

Minnie Opal Wilson 1929

36" x 36" Machine quilted by Shannon Shirley

Kansas Farmer

Tinted linens were popular in the 1930s, and many women of the time experimented with a wide variety of painting techniques. My Grandmother Opal created this set of kitchen towels depicting a jolly farmer and his wife surrounded with wheat stalks. I pieced the borders using vintage brown and green solids into the classic Chicken and Hens pattern. Two sizes of half-square triangles are arranged in a festive frame.

13" x 16" Hand quilted by Doris Bloomer

Helpful hint: Piece your borders first, and trim the linen embroidery to fit the pieced border sizes.

Kansas Farmwife

13" x 16" Hand quilted by Doris Bloomer

Black Magic

Every well-dressed family table was covered by a tablecloth. Utility cloths were often made of printed cotton, and thousands of designs were printed in the 1940s and '50s. Other cloths featured embroidered details, and still others showcased thread skills and cut-work designs. This crisp white Cut Work tablecloth was layered with black to showcase the linen, and finely quilted by Dusty Farrell with his signature feathers.

45" x 45" Long Arm quilted by Dusty Farrell

Days of the Week Towels

In the era of "decorate everything," hundreds of sewing patterns were created and marketed to American women. Some of the most popular patterns were for sets of seven kitchen towels, that depict time-management tasks for each day of the week. Often, towel sets gave suggestions for daily activities that reflected the strong work ethic and attention-to-detail that enabled a busy home to run smoothly.

This set of embroidered tea towels features a sassy black child, reminiscent of the popular Pickaninny character of the time. On Monday this adorable child is Happy, and on Wednesday she is Lazy. By Saturday she is Wise, and for Sunday the towel reads, "But Mammy on a Sunday is an Angel in Disguise."

Seven Days of Sunshine

I could not resist pulling out my wallet when I found this bright set of appliquéd towels in a Kentucky antique shop. Each of the solid towels features an industrious girl with appliquéd pants and a wide-brimmed hat. Her week is spent washing, ironing and at the market. On Sunday, she heads to church. The bright blocks were set with unifying black cotton, and various lengths of leftover strips created a scrappy border.

Detail

45" x 45" Long Arm quilted by Erin Underwood

A Chef in the Kitchen

There was not a needlework skill that my grandmother, Opal Wilson, did not master. She embraced every craft technique that was ever invented and tried as many as she could afford. In addition to her tatted, crocheted and quilted pieces, we treasure her handcrafted jewelry and her curled tin ornaments created from recycled soda cans. She made our Barbie clothes and created every stuffed animal we ever loved. One of her favorite mediums was painted textiles. When Tri-Chem introduced their line of paint tubes in the 1950s, she was hooked and created dozens of painted designs. Later, she would entertain her grandchildren, as we were allowed to play with her paints and create our own masterpieces.

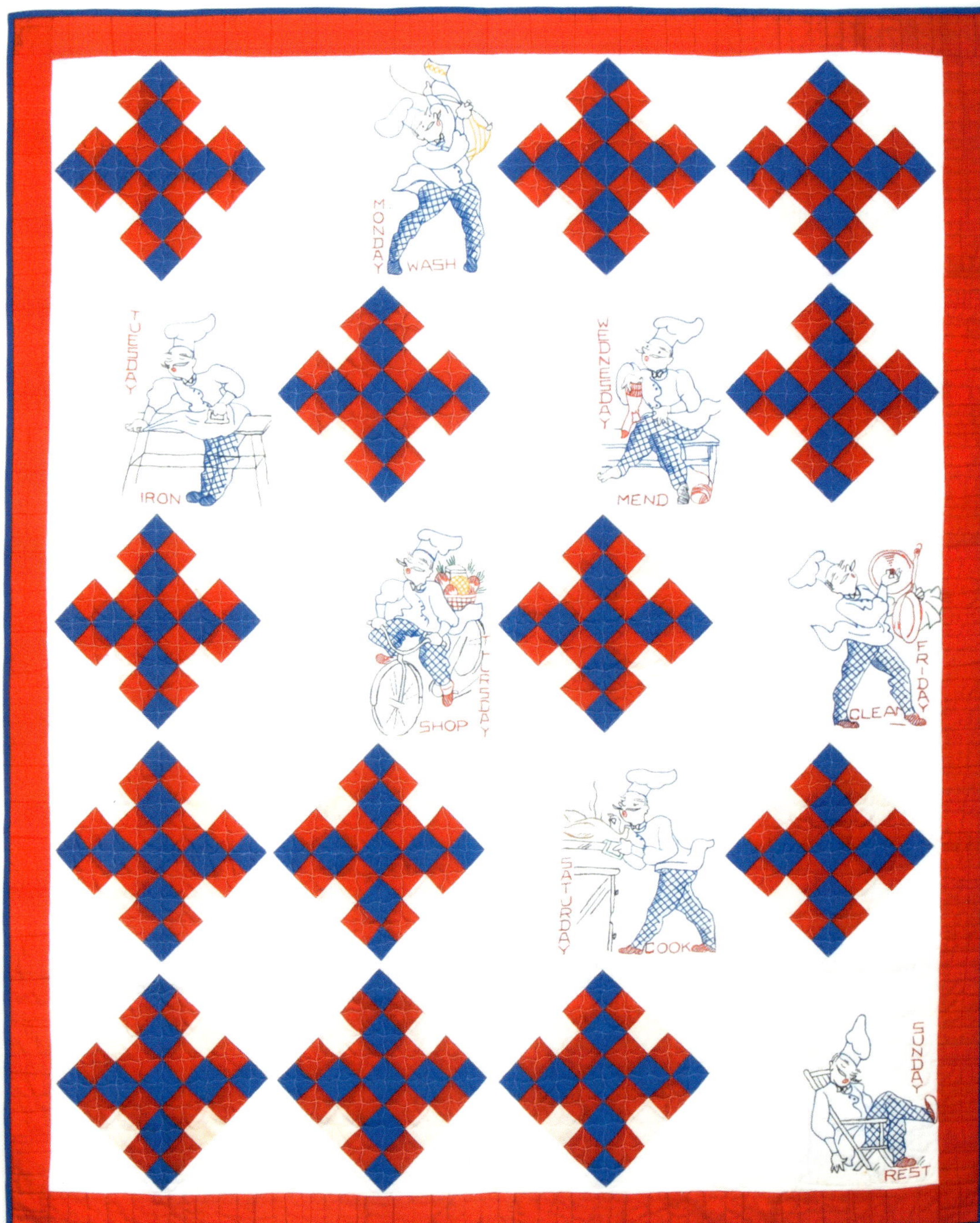

44" x 56" Long Arm quilted by Myrna Ficken

Opal painted a days-of-the-week set of French Chefs using Tri-Chem paints in the 1960s. She never used this set of towels nor was she a fancy cook. She could however, feed an army, and her Peanut Butter Cookies will always be a family favorite! I paired these productive chefs with fragments of a red, white and blue Irish Chain quilt top from the 1940s.

Hint: Setting the pieced blocks on point with oversized triangles allowed me to trim the blocks to the needed size and compensate for the discrepancies in size of the vintage 25-patch blocks. Add larger triangles on each side of your square and then trim to fit.

Detail of *A Chef in the Kitchen*

Nana's Napkins

In the 1950s, my mother, Corene Say Wilson, starting embroidering a set of preprinted napkins with a matching tablecloth. The four napkins were beautifully embroidered, but life interrupted and the tablecloth was never completed. When I received the set a few years ago, the threaded needle was still in the fabric and the label was still attached! I appliquéd the four napkins onto a coordinating background and then appliquéd this unit onto the linen tablecloth to showcase the elegant scalloped edge. There are three layers of appliqué that were each cut away to reduce bulk. The unfinished center of the tablecloth was pieced into the backing, as I wanted to incorporate all of the embroidery possible. Teri Lucas machine quilted this sentimental piece with high contrast thread and dense quilting.

44" x 44" Machine quilted by Teri Lucas

Detail of quilt back

Appliqu*é* in progress

A single napkin

Chapter Two

Dresser Scarves and Embroidered Linens

Most young girls in the 1930s were taught needle skills before they went to school. My mother, Corene Crissie Say, was the third girl born to a struggling, Kansas, farm family. She was taught to sew at an early age and was encouraged to create textiles that were used in the home. Kitchen linens, dresser scarves, pillow cases, and tablecloths were all embellished with embroidery stitches. As my grandmother would say, "We may not have had much but we made it look pretty."

Embroidered linens were used throughout the home in every imaginable way. Tabletops were covered to prevent scratches, chairs were draped to protect them from dirt, fabric bags held clothes, and pillows provided decorative comfort. Thousands of designs were available through magazines, mail order, and purchased patterns. Some designs were iron-on transfers, some were traced, and others were pre-printed on linen or cotton.

Family linen, maker unknown

The Say family, 1945

Grandma Kay Loved Purple

My Grandma Kay had the proverbial green thumb, and it seemed as though there was nothing that she could not coax to grow. She had huge vegetable gardens, an enchanted strawberry patch, and every type of flower one can imagine. As a child, I remember a small porch and sun room packed with beautiful African Violets. Grandma Kay loved and nurtured all the varieties. Is it any wonder that her favorite color was purple?

I was the fortunate recipient of three damaged dresser scarves that had belonged to Grandma Kay. I paired the fragments with purple feed sack fabric and incorporated the undamaged bits into this pieced wall hanging. After I completed the top, I discovered that one of the purple feed sacks had belonged to my great-grandmother, Rose Pickering. I used tiny vintage buttons to secure the edges of the scarves and preserve the delicate crocheted edging.

28" x 28" Hand quilted by Didi Salvatierra

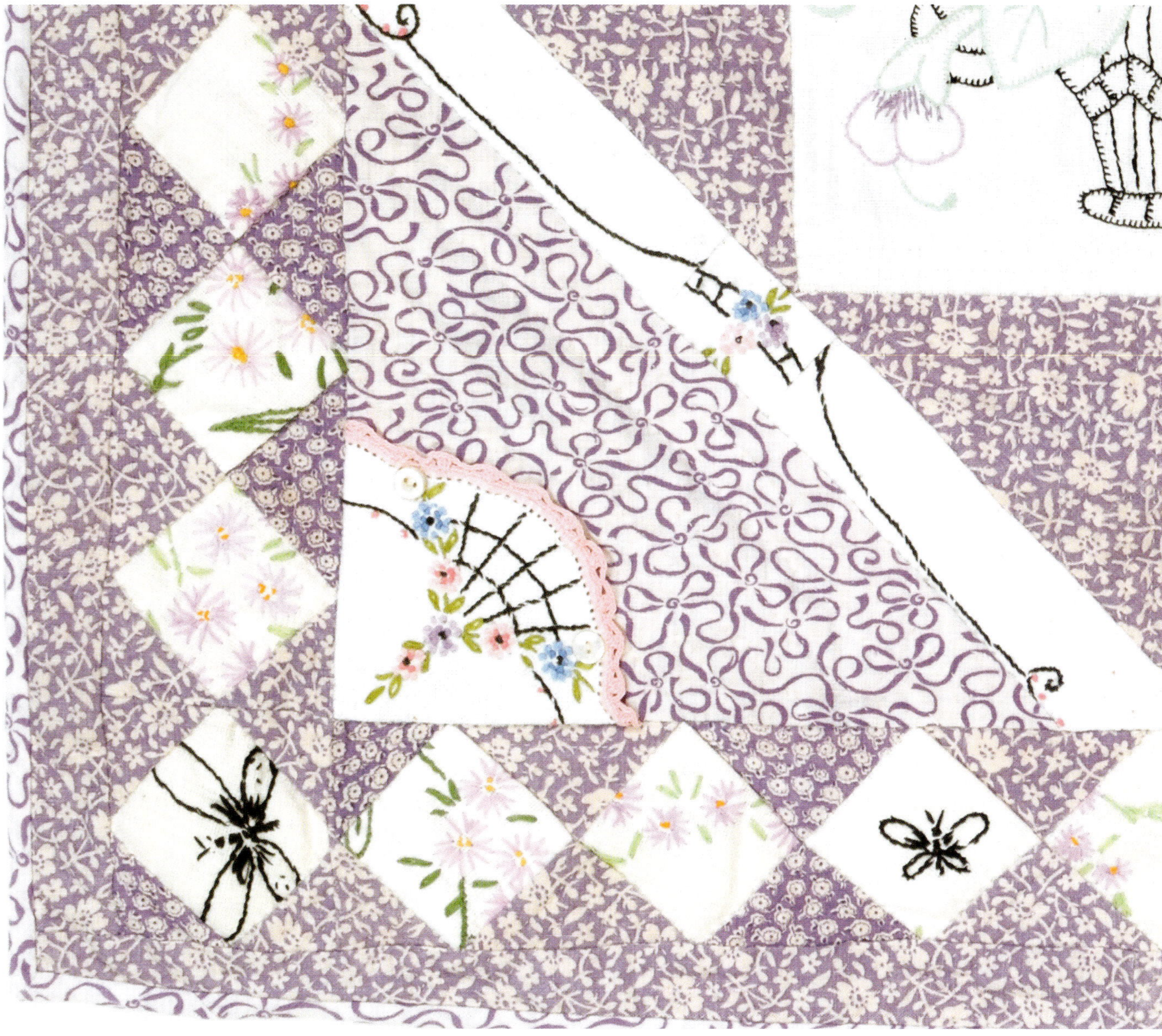

Detail of quilt corner

Hint: Corner treatments are a great way to showcase the edge of a treasured linen. After your piece has been quilted, pin the linen section in place and catch the cut edges in the binding to secure. Fasten the crocheted edges with small buttons or hidden stitches.

Tea Party

My great-great-grandparents, Charles and Emma Say, emigrated from England in 1866. They raised their family in Junction City, Kansas, where six of their eleven children survived to adulthood. Charles was a brick mason, oil painter, and lover of his English teas. This 18 ½ x 28-inch wall hanging celebrates this "civilized" side of my family. Fragments of a damaged kitchen towel were paired with vintage fabric from my Grandma Kay's collection. My mother remembers curtains created from this fabric that hung at the farmhouse she grew up in. It is now in the collection of Charles and Emma's great-great-granddaughter, Karen Wilson Mitchell.

Charles and Amelia Say, 1915

18" x 28" Hand quilted
by Kathy Hastings

The butterfly was a popular motif in the 1930s and 1940s. We find an overwhelming number of appliqué and embroidery patterns that celebrate this favorite insect. Wings and antenna seem to be far more amenable than anything with legs! Some versions were far more delicate than others. This whimsical set of blocks looks more like reindeer than butterflies.

Wings of Hope

The butterflies in this small wall hanging were salvaged from a dresser scarf that had been damaged by burn holes. It was surrounded by an unappealing orange and black crocheted edge treatment. Three-inch blocks were fussy-cut, to showcase the butterfly motifs, and set on-point with fabric from a coarse, brown, feed sack. I pieced the border using tiny, half-square triangles created from additional feed sack fragments. It is now in the collection of Kay's granddaughter, Nancy Wilson Buckler.

13" x 17" Hand quilted by Doris Bloomer

Blessings in Purple

25" x 25" Machine quilted by Stacy Kohler

These two quilts were created from two ends of a dresser scarf that my mother embroidered in 1945. The tinted paintings of the 1930s were now embellished with outline embroidery stitches. This outline stitch was one of the first taught to novice needleworkers, who simply stitched along the lines they were given.

Corene Say 1950

I chose to finish these identical embroideries in two different ways. In this first wall hanging, the embroidery was bordered with fabric from a recycled purple shirt and embellished with pieces of a Double Wedding Ring quilt top. The yellow version is bordered with triple sashing fragments rescued from a family quilt top. It is surrounded by fragments of a 1930s Grandmothers Flower Garden top and backed with the same fabric used in my Tea Party quilt.

Blessings in Yellow

25" x 25" Machine quilted by Stacy Kohler

Remembering Dee

This small quilt was created when I paired a floral embroidered dresser scarf with fragments of a skirt that belonged to my mother's sister, Delores Say Mickey. The corners were cropped when I realized that I needed several more inches of fabric to make the borders fit. Sometimes necessity really is the key to success. It is now in the collection of Dee's daughter, Lynette Mickey Kieffer.

18" x 27" Hand quilted by Kathy Hastings

Black Flowers 1934

This quilt was created from a Vogue Needlecraft embroidered pillow top that was expertly stitched, but never completed. The manufacturer's information, stamped at the edge of the embroidery, indicates that it was pattern #47. It was finished simply when I set the motif on point with vintage green sashing, new black fabric, and a floral cotton from the 1950s.

Hint: Feel free to mix and match fabrics from different eras. Complimentary colors can be found that span the generations. Think outside your normal range!

33" x 33" Machine quilted by Karen Dever and Cyndi Souder

Party Time

This jaunty pup is definitely ready to spread some cheer! The tinted embroidery undoubtedly celebrates the end of Prohibition in 1933, as the gentleman offers a drink from his newly flowing keg. I added a fabric flange for a pop of color and set the embroidery with a wide, black border that is appliquéd with fragments of a Double Wedding Ring quilt top. This non-traditional placement of the wedding ring pieces adds to the playfulness of the piece.

30" x 30" Machine quilted by Merry May

28" x 28" Machine quilted by Jane Hamilton

May I Have This Dance?

I fell in love with this pair of dancing cats whose maker chose to appliqué festive clothes where we would normally find tinted fabric. The embroidery was set with a double flange and bordered with fragments of a Grandmother's Flower Garden quilt top.

Hint: A flange is a great way to add a pop of color to a piece. One inch strips are folded in half and inserted into the seam. Sew the folded fabric along the seam line and then piece as normal. To hide the stitches, move the needle on your machine one step to the left.

Help With the Laundry

I was given this embroidered laundry bag that showcases two Scottie dogs who are ready to help with the chores. My mother remembers this textile from her childhood, but the details of who might have made it are long gone. The Scottie dog motifs were very popular after President Franklin D Roosevelt introduced his Scottie named Fala to America in 1940.

The top of the laundry bag was badly damaged, so I folded it under and appliquéd the entire piece to a black background. The use of solid black lets the colors pop and coordinated well with the embroidery work. This central unit was bordered with fragments from an unfinished quilt top that had been made my great-grandmother, Crissie Say in the 1930s (see next page).

Harry and Crissie Say, 1940

Quilt top created by Crissie Say, 1930

A Pretty Pink Bow

As women continued to work outside the home in the 1960s, textile manufacturers began to market pre-embroidered linens. This pink pillowcase was an example of one of the countless items consumers could choose from. I collaborated with Stephanie Farrell to design this sweet lap quilt. A dark pink fabric bow was layered under the pillow top, and this shadow technique coordinates perfectly with the pink embroidered bows, the original scalloped edge, and the pieced pink and white border. I added a contemporary polka dot fabric for the backing.

39" x 35" Long Arm quilted by Dusty Farrell

Hint: To create a shadow image, layer a dark strong shape of fabric under a pale layer. Quilt around the shape to make it stand out.

Chapter Three

Handkerchiefs, Doilies, and More

Handkerchiefs have been used for centuries as objects of personal hygiene, symbols of social standing, and decorative fashion accessories. In 1924, facial tissue, as it is known today, was introduced as a means to remove make-up. Early advertisements linked Kleenex to Hollywood makeup departments and sometimes included endorsements from movie stars who used tissues to remove their theatrical makeup with cold cream. It was the customers who started to use Kleenex as a disposable handkerchief, and by the 1930s Kleenex was being marketed with the slogan "Don't Carry A Cold In Your Pocket."

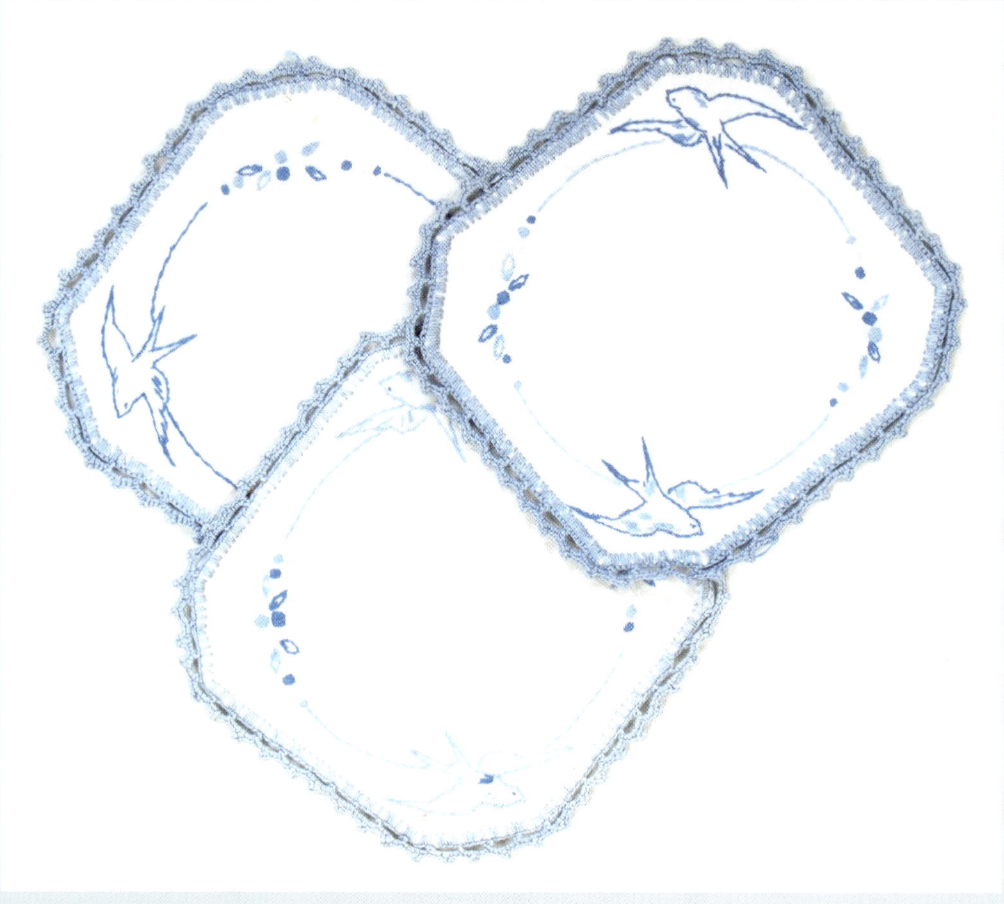

Still, after the introduction of disposable tissues, American women continued to carry and collect handkerchiefs. Many were manufactured as decorative accents, soldiers sent them back to their girlfriends as mementos, and others were sold as souvenirs. These inexpensive linens were frequently given as gifts and their popularity soared during the economic hardships of the 1930s and '40s. My grandmothers were not wealthy women, yet each had drawers and boxes full of beautiful handkerchiefs.

A Little Black Bow

I wanted to showcase this pretty handkerchief that belonged to my Grandma Opal. I set it on point on a white background and quilted it in waves, in an assortment of thread colors. Wendy Hill developed this style of quilting that encourages the use of simple flowing lines to add depth and definition. The composition allowed the handkerchief to be the focus of this small quilt. I used scraps of a Grandmothers Flower Garden top for the backing.

Opal Cummins 1932

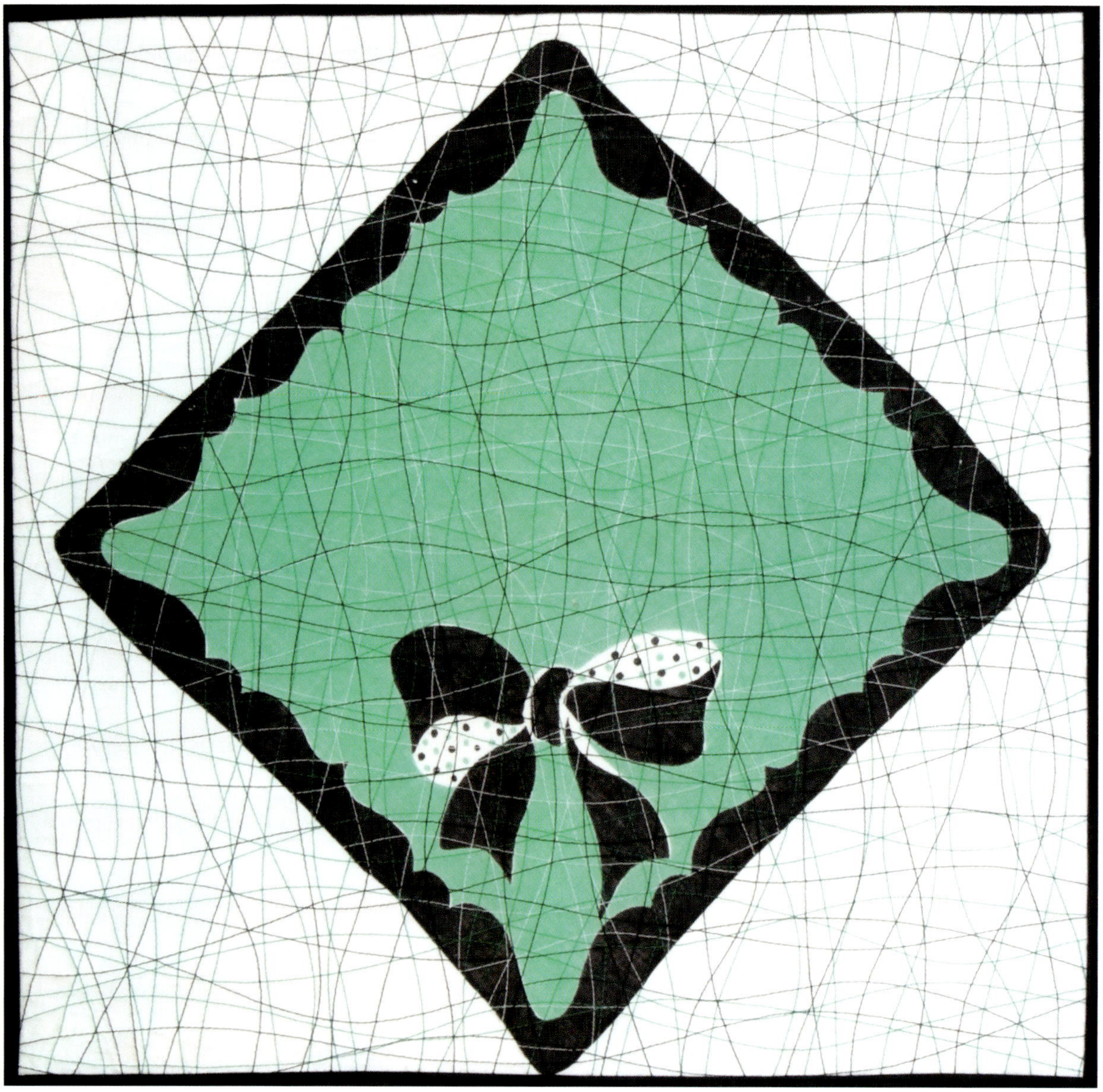

18" x 18" Machine quilted by Mary Kerr

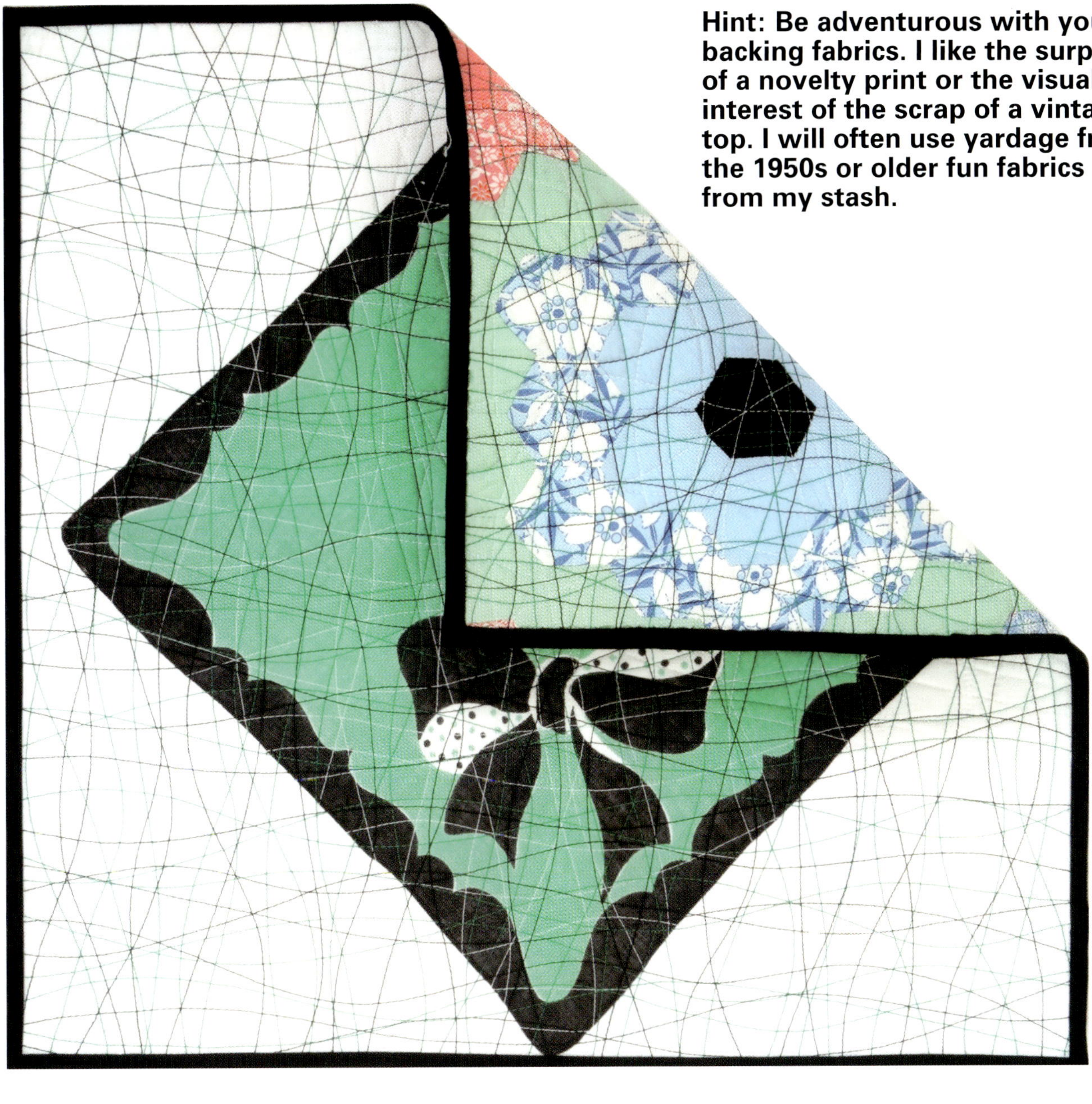

Hint: Be adventurous with your backing fabrics. I like the surprise of a novelty print or the visual interest of the scrap of a vintage top. I will often use yardage from the 1950s or older fun fabrics from my stash.

A Green Rose Pillow

This pillow was constructed in the same manner as A Little Black Bow. A bright handkerchief was set on a pink background with Wendy Hill threadwork as the quilting. Crisp white shirting was added as the back to create a decorative pillow.

22" x 22" Machine quilted by Mary Kerr

Hint: Finish your pillows by using an old shirt as the backing. With right sides together, stitch the quilted pillow top and the shirt front on all 4 sides. Unbutton the shirt front and turn the right sides through the buttonholes. Press well and stitch 1 – 2 inches from edge to create a decorative flange. Insert your pillow form and button the placket closed. This is recycling at its finest!

Train Ride Pillow

My mother-in-law, Mary Elizabeth Hennighan Kerr, was not a quilter. She appreciated my quilting, encouraged our hobbies, and tolerated her husband's love of trains. After her death in 2005, I was given a scarf that had been in her collection.

It was red, white and black with a celebration of trains. I quilted it with coordinating threads and backed it with a recycled, bright red jacket front.

Mary Elizabeth Hennighan 1945

28" x 28" Machine quilted by Mary Kerr

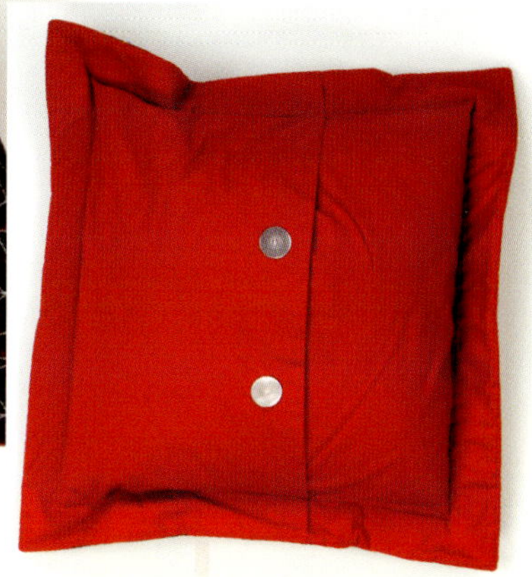

Back view

Doilies

Doilies are small table coverings crocheted with linen or cotton thread. The open-stitch work allows the surface of the table or chair underneath to show through. They are decorative, but also have the utilitarian role of protecting furniture from scratches caused by everyday items we place on tables. Numerous crochet patterns for doilies and table coverings were published in the first part of the 20th century; it was a wildly popular sewing technique in American culture. Most of the women in my family learned to crochet as young girls.

Opal's Rainbow

22" x 22" Machine quilted by Mary Kerr

I love using doilies in my home, but a girl can have only so much table surface on which to display things! I had numerous additional pieces that I wanted to showcase by incorporating them into small wall hangings. This bright doily was created by my Grandmother Opal in the 1950s. I created a base by piecing scraps of a Snowball quilt top on point around vintage green cotton. After the base unit was quilted and bound, I machine appliquéd the doily to the quilt using coordinating thread.

Hint: To create a quilted frame wall hanging, first determine the finished size you will need for your focus needlework. Add large triangles to set it on point, additional borders, and quilt as desired. After this unit is complete, attach your needlework with invisible stitches.

A Star from Norton

My Great-Aunt, Nellie Cummins, was my grandmother's sister. She was the eleventh of fifteen children, and the only sibling who never married. She lived with various family members throughout her life in Norton, Kansas.

Aunt Nellie was a talented needlewoman who always had a quilting needle or crochet hook in her hand. I created this wall hanging to showcase a large star doily that she crocheted in the 1970s. I framed a dark green square of contemporary fabric with two large vintage blocks that had been cut in half.

29" x 29" Long Arm quilted by Sharon Denston

Nellie Cummins 1932

Cutwork Pillow

This pillow was created to showcase a cut-work doily that was machine produced for decorative use in the 1970s. I formed a base for this doily by machine quilting a fragment of a damaged nine-patch top from about 1900. The cut-work piece was then machine appliquéd onto the pillow top using coordinating thread. I recycled a well-loved denim shirt for the back.

18" x 24" Machine quilted by Mary Kerr

Back view

Hint: Damaged areas of many textiles can be layered to hide the flaws. The top used in my cut-work pillow was worn, yet the flaw is unnoticeable when hidden under the doily.

Chapter Four

Clothing

Articles of clothing evoke all types of memories: a favorite dress that a loved one wore, a style that was unique to the owner, a treasured remembrance from when our babies were young, or a memento of high school days. Deciding what to do with old clothing is hard, and our options in the past have been limited to giving it away or storing it in a closet, trunk or drawer. Creating a quilt that incorporates these pieces of clothing allows us to preserve the memorable fabric in a quilt that can be displayed and enjoyed.

These two dresses are indicative of some of the pieces that could easily be incorporated into quilted textiles. The black housedress is circa 1900 and the orange striped dress is from the 1940s.

Kansas Therapy

When the contents of my grandparents' home were sold at auction, I was able to purchase a number of items that had special meaning to me. I bid on fabrics, quilt blocks, unfinished projects, clothes, and a dozen jars of buttons. One of the pieces was a housedress that my mother remembers playing dress-up in when she was a child. It was created from dark blue Indigo fabric in about 1900 and featured rows and rows of tiny pleats across the bodice. The skirt was worn and there were extensive areas of fading. I carefully removed all the stitching, and pieced Monkey Wrench blocks and a border from all of the available fabric. This memory quilt was hand-quilted in an appropriate Kansas sunflower design.

Detail

Hint: Do not be afraid to piece your fabric! Some of the blocks in this quilt contain more than 20 pieces, as I worked to incorporate as much fabric as possible into the quilt. The challenge was part of the therapy!

47" x 65" Hand quilted by Doris Bloomer

Always Aletha

My great-grandmother, Francis Antis Laffoon Cummins, was married in 1904. John William Cummins was a widower who had eight children, the oldest of whom was just six years younger than his new bride. John was twenty-one years older than Francis, and the family remembers that she only ever called him "Mr. Cummins."

My great-aunt, Aletha Virginia Cummins, was the youngest daughter born to Francis and John Cummins. She and her twin brother were the fourteenth and fifteenth children in the family. Before the babies were a month old, this only son died and a blanket of sadness descended on the family.

24" x 36" Hand quilted by Dawn Jolin

Back detail

29" x 42" Hand quilted by Arlene Troiano

Detail of Grandpa's *Pockets #1*, back view

Grandpa's Pockets #2

The second quilt was pieced in vertical rows using unique blocks from early 1900. The blocks were set with a light blue period fabric that was recycled from a damaged quilt top. And yes, I still have on pocket remaining that waits patiently to be made into a memory quilt.

44" x 44" Hand quilted by Dawn Jolin

Linwood High, 1954

In 1954, my father, James William Wilson, graduated from Linwood Rural High School in Linwood, Kansas. There were six students in his graduating class! As my father says, "The class of 1954 was known for its quality rather than its numbers." They still keep in contact with each other and will celebrate their 60th reunion in 2014.

I "borrowed" his Varsity Letter and class tie to create this small wall hanging that celebrates the purple and gold of Linwood High. Tinted embroidery figures were salvaged from a damaged pillow top and applied with fusible web to the purple back of a cutter quilt base. Buttons, a buckle, a locker key, and old pins from my family collection were attached by hand.

15" x 20" Quilted by Mary Kerr

Detail, *Linwood High*, 1954

Hint: Be creative when attaching items that are too precious to cut up. I did not want to damage this special tie so I knotted it as usual and stitched the ends with long basting stitches. The top of the tie loops over in the 3-dimensional design.

Chapter Five

Buttons and Stuff

All of the women in my family were savers, collectors of things that might possibly be needed again. This was the mentality of the generation who grew up during the Depression era; waste not, want not! Nothing went to waste and all items might possibly be repurposed to fill a need. Tins were filled, jars were collected, and boxes were accumulated. Each of these receptacles are emptied I feel as if I am on a treasure hunt as each of these receptacles are emptied, investigated and repurposed. I was thrilled to find that many of these items are small enough to be incorporated into a quilt. If I can determine a way to attach it to fabric, it is fair game for one of my quilts.

Ben and Nellie Say, 1930

Detail of *Baby Blue Too* (see page 63)

Home

Both of my Grandmothers had button tins and boxes of sewing ephemera. I have been the fortunate recipient of all their sewing tools, and literally thousands of wonderful buttons of all shapes, colors and sizes. This quilt was created when I framed a sentimental embroidery with two interlocking squares of buttons. The base is a fragment of an indigo Four Patch quilt from 1890 that had been damaged beyond repair. The embroidered linen was bordered with red cotton, set asymmetrically, and machine quilted in simple waves. Then I added an envelope backing that was turned and top-stitched in place. After this, I attached two frames of buttons—one featuring antique white buttons and the other is grey. Heavy thread and a big needle helped create this special wall hanging.

24" x 24" Machine quilted by Mary Kerr

Detail

Baby Blue Too

This compilation quilt incorporates a sweet little blue romper, fragments of a 1930s Grandmother's Flower Garden quilt top, vintage tatting, porcelain doll parts, and buttons, LOTS of buttons. The romper was hand-stitched to a quilted base, providing a palate for a waterfall of buttons and doll parts (I told you they saved everything!). An edging of tatted lace made by my Grandmother Opal was inserted around one corner.

13" x 17" Hand and machine quilted by Mary Kerr

Hint: An envelope backing is a great way to add a crisp clean edge to your quilt. With right sides together, stitch the quilted top and the backing on all 4 sides. To turn, cut a small slit 2-3 inches down from the top edge of the backing fabric and turn your quilt through this slit. Only cut through the backing fabric. This opening will be covered by the hanging sleeve. Press well after turning and top-stitch the edges if desired. All hand stitching to attach items should be completed after the quilt has been turned.

Dancing to My Drum

This quilt was created in 2008, when I participated in a local guild challenge with Cabin Branch Quilters of Woodbridge, Virginia. This was the "Quilts of Good Fortune" challenge. Each of us was given a fortune cookie sentiment to interpret into a contemporary quilt.

My fortune said, "What would you do if you had no fear?" My artist statement read, "I have made many quilts for others and numerous quilts in honor of those who I love. As I get caught up in the business and search to find my place in today's quilting community, I find that I rarely take time to create just for me. Knowing I could not fail gives me the freedom to listen to my heart and its own special joy. I have used vintage fabrics, antique pieces, family photos and button embellishments." This is a quilt that celebrates ME!

18" x 24" Hand and machine quilted by Mary Kerr

Family linens and sewing ephemera were stitched to a cutter quilt base creating a collage of neutral colors that surrounds the black dancer. I used articles from both Grandmothers and a crocheted coin purse that had belonged to my great-grandmother, Francis Laffoon Cummins.

Julia Louise Say Hatten, 1905

Everything Opal

My Grandma Opal died in 2007, at the age of ninety-five. After her funeral, I was given several tins of "stuff" from her house: an eclectic collection of jewelry, metal fragments, fabric scraps, newspaper clippings, buttons, and more. I created this wall hanging the week following her death to remember all those many facets of my grandmother that made her the special woman she was. I incorporated some of her painted linens and tapestry scraps from her upholstery business. I added a crocheted dress front, Bakelite buckles, a small key, and a tiny miraculous medal. I included newspaper clippings from a 1947 issue of *The Kansas City Star* to honor the many quilts she created in her lifetime. Lastly, I added the holy card from her service and added more buttons. I treasure our time together and I welcomed the opportunity to create a quilt that would help preserve some of my memories of Opal. This quilt is now in the collection of her oldest son, James Wilson.

Four Generations, 1937: Sarah Pennington, Allie Wilson, Harry Wilson and Jim Wilson

Hint: Secure paper and cardboard to the front of your quilt with buttons. Layer the paper on top of the quilt and carefully stitch the buttons in place through all the layers. Quilts that incorporate paper can be fragile, and should be used only for display.

13" x 17" Hand and machine quilted by Mary Kerr

Hindsight

In 2009, Cabin Branch Quilt Guild celebrated its 20th Anniversary with a "20-20" challenge. This collage quilt incorporates 20 different pieces of family memorabilia. The items include a 1930s signature block, handkerchiefs, a felt needle case, a church key, buttons, and even a bra extender.

Cora Hayes (see her name on the quilt) was my grandmother's aunt. She was a prolific quilter who enjoyed sharing signature blocks with her friends and family.

20" x 20" Hand and machine quilted by Mary Kerr

Quilt detail

Hint: When creating a collage piece, work with your digital camera. After you decide where everything will be placed, take pictures! You will need to work from the base up to attach your items. The photos you take will be your own personal road map.

Chapter Six

Working with Vintage Fabrics

While some vintage fabrics are in pristine condition, most of the pieces that are passed on to us have been exposed to a variety of conditions, abuse and misuse. Ripped seams and frayed embroidery are common, while other pieces are stained or torn. I have seen dresser scarves with burn holes and fabric that is riddled with mouse holes. Some of the damage can be repaired. One can carefully repair the pieces and clean the textile. Decorative edging can be reattached and separating seams can be resewn. Holes can be patched and missing fabric replaced.

This chapter presents another option: use a portion of the vintage textile to create a new quilt that honors the memory of those who made the textile. Realize that the piece has served well, but seen better days. By incorporating fragments into a contemporary quilt, new life is breathed into the textile, allowing it to continue to be appreciated, enjoyed, and, yes, remembered.

Dirt and stains

Each of us has our own comfort level when we address the issue of dirt and stains. I see most stains as well-deserved age spots and freckles, but I do prefer to work with clean fabric. If you are bothered by the condition of your textile, please take the time to wash it before you start playing with it. Most fabrics do well if they are gently hand-washed. A gentle soak in a quality quilt wash (there are many on the market) removes surface dirt and some stains. Restoration is the best product for removing overall yellowing. There are always risks when cleaning antique textiles, but I would rather address the issues at the start.

Old-fashioned Safeguard soap will remove smoke smells from fabric. Unwrap a bar of white soap, wrap it in a white paper towel, and place the soap and offending textile in a sealed plastic bag for two to three days. Repeat as needed until the odor is removed. The bar of soap can be reused indefinitely.

Dissecting the Textile

If you choose to take your textile apart, a good ripper is your best friend. The goal is to save as much material as possible so you can use the fabric and trim in a new and exciting way. For both hand- and machine-stitched seams, gently remove the stitches from the underside of the fabric by snipping every other thread. You do not want to rip the seam or pull a long thread; both of these methods will distort the fabric.

Decorative edging can be removed by carefully cutting the thread that attaches it to the textile. Historically, most edgings were created as yardage and later attached to a fabric base.

Embroidered motifs can be cut from a textile in any size or shape. This is a great way to work around damaged areas and still use the decorative motifs. If working with a thin or stretchy fabric, either cut with the grain of the fabric or reinforce the textile with a light interfacing.

Quilt fragment used in *Blessings in Yellow* (see page 33)

An odd shape can easily be cut from a textile if you first iron it to a fusible interfacing. After the piece is attached to your quilt, cover the edges with decorative stitches or secure them with quilting stitches.

Detail of *Linwood High 1954* (see page 59)

Detail of *A Rooster from Linwood* (see page 15)

Incorporating vintage blocks, tops and fragments

Several of the quilts in this book also feature vintage blocks and tops that have been recycled from unfinished or damaged textiles. These vintage blocks are not for the perfectionist quilter, as they were often left undone for good reason. One has to understand that the sensibilities of past eras are not necessarily our own.

Many blocks were not finished because of inferior workmanship. Check the seam allowances to ensure that the pieces will not separate as they are pressed and sewn into a new project. If there is not a quarter-inch of fabric around the outside of the design, the overall image will be distorted.

A number of the blocks we work with are not square and they vary in size. Some of us are not bothered by these issues, while others prefer to remake the offending design. The choice is up to you.

Poor quality fabrics can distort the quilt pieces, causing the blocks to stretch or pull out of shape. If the block does not lay flat on your worktable, it may bow in your finished project unless you take extra care to correct the problems. Thin fabrics can be reinforced with interfacing or another layer of cotton.

Tips to Remember

- Any textile can be incorporated into a memory quilt.
- Vintage and contemporary fabrics mix well.
- It is okay to combine vintage fabrics from multiple eras.
- Embellishments can be used to cover a multitude of flaws.
- If you can attach an item to your quilt, it works.
- Ignore the quilt police, they are not invited to your party.
- Give yourself permission to play.
- Think outside your normal box.
- Document your story.
- Relax, enjoy, and create what makes your heart sing!

Detail of *Blessings in Purple* (see page 32) Quilted by Stacy Kohler

Labels and Documentation

As contemporary quilters, we have been told over and over that each of our quilts needs to be labeled. At minimum, we are instructed to provide the maker's name, the quilter's name, and the date the quilt was created. There are a number of ways to create these labels and they range from the very basic to elaborately embellished envelopes of data.

When are working with memory pieces, we have an obligation to provide as much information as possible. I encourage my students to document all they know about the textile in order to establish a connection with the intended recipient. If I am creating a gift for my son, using embroidered linen made by his great-grandmother, that background information should be included. I will remember where the items came from, but I cannot expect my children or future generations to remember the details if I do not provide them.

I have frequently created labels using vintage blocks. I apply a fusible web to the back and write the information directly on the block using fabric pens. I list the maker of the vintage linen, when I created the piece, who quilted it and why I was inspired to make this particular memory quilt. The two labels shown here are found on the back of Grandpas Pockets #2 and Baby Blue Too.

Another wonderful option is to use photo transfer software to incorporate a picture of the maker into your label. A vintage photo can be scanned into your computer and supporting details can be added and printed onto photo-transfer paper. I frame this label with strips of fabric and appliqué it to the back of the quilt. This technique allows me to pass on the information and special sentiments to the recipient and future generations.

Detail of *Grandpa's Pockets #2* (see page 58)

Detail of *Baby Blue Too* (see page 63)

Back detail of *Wings of Hope* (see page 31)

Variations in Quilting

Quilting stitches are the glue that holds a quilt together. These decorative stitches add definition, dimension, and another layer of design to a textile. Finishing a quilt is an age-old dilemma, and many people scratch their heads to find the right way. The very words "quilt as desired" strike fear into the heart of even the most experienced quilter. Fortunately, there are as many ways to finish a quilt as there are quilters who work on them. Each individual brings their own talents and taste to the worktable.

I have finished quilts with almost every technique available. I love the look of hand quilting for some pieces, but others sing loudest with dense machine quilting. I enjoy the movement of wavy lines in Wendy Hill's quilting technique and I love the flow of an undulating feather.

I have chosen to have all but a few of the quilts shown in this book finished by another person. I hand-quilt when time allows and I have experimented with a variety of machine quilting techniques. I have long known, however, that there are members of my quilting community who are far more talented as quilters that I am. My love is in the inspiration and design, so now I ask others to quilt my pieces. The name of each quilter is listed prominently on my quilt label because I believe they should be credited in any and all exhibition paperwork. I was thrilled to collaborate with each of these talented artists and my work would not have been the same without the addition of their talent. A list of their contact information can be found in the last pages of this book.

Detail of *Black Magic,* (see page 17) Quilted by Dusty Farrell

Epilogue

My memory quilts have allowed me to discover one more way of passing on the gifts of our family stories. My children will not remember the family members who died before they were born, however they will remember the stories I tell and the textiles that I choose to display in our home. The memories of my family can live on as I breathe new life into objects that would otherwise have stayed in the trunk or dresser drawer. I have been blessed to be able to work with these artifacts from my family and hope to continue inspiring others to create their own special memory pieces.

Detail from *Home* (page 62)

Grandma Opal's Peanut Butter Cookies

1 cup shortening
1 cup white sugar
1 cup brown sugar
2 eggs, beaten
1 cup peanut butter
3 cups flour
2 tsp soda
¼ tsp salt
1 tsp vanilla

Cream sugars and shortening. Add eggs, peanut butter and vanilla. Add dry ingredients and mix well. Form dough into balls a little smaller than English Walnuts. Press flat with a silver fork. Bake at 375 for 10-15 minutes. Enjoy.

Mary, Nancy and Karen Wilson, 1967

Professional Quilters

These are the quilters who I collaborated with who have chosen to be available for hire.

Hand Quilters

Doris Bloomer
Appling, Georgia
hbl0847023@aol.com

Dawn Jolin
Jetersville, Virginia
dljolin@hotmail.com

Didi Salvatierra
Bel Air, Maryland
www.DidiQuilts.com
Didi@DidiQuilts.com

Machine Quilters

Karen Dever
Moorestown, New Jersey
www.karendever.com
njquiltappraisr@aol.com

Jane Hamilton
Unionville, Pennsylvania
www.Janesquilts.com
quiltrjane@aol.com

Teri Lucas
New York, New York
terificreations.wordpress.com
terificreations@gmx.com

Merry May
Tuckahoe, New Jersey
www.MerryMayhem.com
twotonsofbuttons@gmail.com

Shannon Shirley
Woodbridge, Virginia
www.onceinarabbitmoon.com
onceinarabbitmoon@comcast.net

Cyndi Souder
Annandale, Virginia
www.MoonlightingQuilts.com
Cyndi@MoonlightingQuilts.com

Long-arm Quilters

Sharon Denston
Clementon, New Jersey
sdensten@comcast.net

Dustin Farrell
Cambridge Springs, Pennsylvania
www.cscountrystitchin.com
countrystitchin@verizon.net

Myrna Ficken
Spokane, Washington
www.aquilterschoice.com

Stacy Koehler
Swarthmore, Pennsylvania
skoequilt@aol.com

Index

Back of *Blessings in Purple* (see page 32)